KENO WINNER

KENO WINNER

❀

A Guide to Winning at Video Keno

Tom Collins

iUniverse, Inc.
New York Lincoln Shanghai

Keno Winner
A Guide to Winning at Video Keno

iUniverse, Inc.

For information address:
iUniverse, Inc.
2021 Pine Lake Road, Suite 100
Lincoln, NE 68512
www.iuniverse.com

Visit us on the web at www.kenowinner.com

ISBN: 0-595-31574-7

Printed in the United States of America

For my Grandparents,
Harry V Meyer and Lucy Ann Collins
Who in the old days:
Just Loved to Play the Numbers

Contents

❀

Foreword

❀

A note from the author about "A Guide to Winning at Video Keno":

If you like to play Lotto or you enjoy the thrill of matching numbers and winning at Bingo, you will love Video Keno!

Video Keno moves faster than Bingo or the Lottery and without doubt has the very best payouts of any game in the casino. There is no other game in the casino that you can win five-hundred up to ten-thousand dollars and in some cases more, on just a one-nickel, or one-quarter wager.

I am a professional Aircraft Technical Writer working for a major airline for the past fifteen years. During this time, I have authored hundreds of technical procedures and How-To manuals. I am also a long time dedicated Video Keno player, and have had a lot of fun, and a great deal of success playing the game.

At the urging of my friends and family, I was asked to share my winning strategies for Video Keno in a simple to understand, straightforward format.

This guide has intentionally been developed to be read quickly and easily, possibly, as you are on your way to the casino.

If you have only been playing slots up until now, try Video Keno, you will not be disappointed! **Come home a Winner!**

❀

CHAPTER 1

General Description and Play

Video Keno is a Lottery type, computer generated, random number game. It displays a matrix screen in sequence from 1 to 80. The Board is laid out in a box format as shown below.

1	2	3	4	5	6	7	8	9	10
11	12	13	14	15	16	17	18	19	20
21	22	23	24	25	26	27	28	29	30
31	32	33	34	35	36	37	38	39	40

41	42	43	44	45	46	47	48	49	50
51	52	53	54	55	56	57	58	59	60
61	62	63	64	65	66	67	68	69	70
71	72	73	74	75	76	77	78	79	80

Standard Video Keno Board Format

The game is played by the player first wagering from 1 to 50 credits, (for this purpose we will refer to coins wagered as credits regardless of the denomination) and then selecting from 2 to 10 player selected numbers on the touch video screen. Each number selected by the player will automatically be highlighted on the video screen once selected. The player then pushes the start button to begin the game.

The Video Keno machine automatically begins picking and displaying on the video screen, a series of 20 randomly selected numbers, one at a time. The numbers selected by the Video Keno machine are selected by a Random Number Generator (RNG) computer chip. That is securely located inside the Keno machine.

Each number picked by the player and matched by the random numbers displayed on the Keno video screen is called a Hit. Most machines will alert the player to a hit with an audio signal. The machine uses a tone such as a Bing for every number matched. Additionally a highlight is also presented on the Video Screen.

The number of Hits (a random computer match to the player-selected numbers) versus the numbers selected by the player determines the payout and the outcome of that particular game.

The amount of the win is displayed on the left side of the video screen. It is then automatically credited to the players account.

The following example shows seven numbers selected by the player and six of those numbers that have been matched by the computer random selection, for a win of 400 credits.

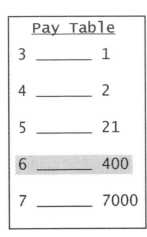

Pay Table	
3 _____	1
4 _____	2
5 _____	21
6 _____	400
7 _____	7000

1	2	3	4	5	6	7	8	9	10
11	12	13	14	15	16	17	18	19	20
21	22	23	24	25	26	27	28	29	30
31	32	33	34	35	36	37	38	39	40
41	42	43	44	X	X	47	48	49	50
51	52	53	54	X	X	57	58	59	60
61	62	63	64	X	X	67	68	69	70
71	72	73	74	75	76	77	78	79	80

HIT X	No HIT

SEVEN NUMBERS PLAYED ("6 Hits = 400 Credits")

Several versions of Video Keno are currently offered in most casinos. The most popular games are:

Video Keno: This is called the Straight Keno play version. This version of the game generally has the highest single payouts, but is considered by most players as the hardest to hit for payouts. The focus of this guide to *Winning at Video Keno* is structured on the Straight Keno play version of the game for the following reason; it generally has the highest payouts.

2/4/6 Keno: This game is a consistent money winner, with small but frequent payouts, although it has relatively low jackpot payouts. The real deciding factor for playing this game or not is that for maximum pay-outs, the minimum credit play is seven credits (coins) per play. 2/4/6 Video Keno can be very expensive to play, even when playing nickels.

Super Way Keno: Identical to the 2/4/6 Keno Games in play, except nine numbers are selected by the player instead of six. Super Way Keno is also a consistent small payout game and the same wagers of seven credits (coins) are needed for the maximum number of pay lines. Although Super Way Keno has substantial jackpot payouts, you must hit at least eight out of nine numbers for a major jackpot payout.

Note: 2/4/6 Keno and Super Way Keno are both excellent Video Keno games to win consistent small payouts. The problem is the relatively large wager makes them uneconomical to play for long periods. Remember all games of chance in the casino are odds favored to the house. Extended play at any casino game will make you a consistent Loser. My advise, if you like the action of the 2/4/6 Keno or Super Way Keno, play only for short periods of time and be happy with the small victories. This means take the money and run. Go home a Winner, not a Loser.

Super Keno: Is one of the most popular, and possibly the worst Video Keno game to play in the casino. Super Keno is played the same as Straight Keno with one exception; the first number randomly picked by the Video Keno machine acts as a multiplier to the pay table.

This may sound at first like a real bonus to the player, but is in fact what I call a Hook that adds a gimmick to the game at the price of the pay table. If the machine randomly selects one of your picked numbers on the very first number displayed, a Lightening Bolt is displayed on the screen, followed by an audio clap of thunder that usually startles you with its intensity and volume.

I see many people playing this game and laughing at the Lightening Bolt display followed by the audio thunder. The shame of it is, unless the multiplier is in effect, the payout for a jackpot can be as low as 1/3rd the amount of a Straight Keno jackpot.

Many times I've seen a six out of six win, or even a seven out of seven win by a player who only collects $250.00 to $700.00 for a single quarter wager. The same win on a Straight Keno game pays $400.00 to $1,750.00 for the same twenty-five cent wager.

In all fairness, I have seen a few jackpots paid with the Lightening Bolt multiplier in effect which makes the win a hefty sum to take home. Although more often than not, I have seen Super Keno players make that big hit that should pay thousands of dollars, but in reality only pays a few hundred dollars. My advice, stay away from Super Keno there are much better games to play.

Progressive Video Keno: Some casinos are featuring large jackpot Progressive Video Keno games. Most of the games are based on Straight Video Keno and offer some substantial jackpots. Watch out for the low-end payouts. In the quest for a progressive jackpot, it may cost you hundreds if you win on a seven out of seven, or a seven out of eight. The Progressive Jackpots are usually paid only on an eight out of eight through ten out of ten win.

Assorted Keno Games: Like all other video games, different casinos have different versions and types of video gaming devices.

If you happen to run across an interesting version of Video Keno, before you put in one coin, measure the payout against the standard payouts that we are looking for. Do not play low payout Video Keno machines. They are no easier to win on than the much higher payout machines that are readily available.

The preferred payouts we are looking for are covered in Chapter 3 of this guide. Remember, you are there to **WIN MONEY** not make a donation to the casinos operating budget. They make enough money from the uninformed player.

Note: For those of you with a technical interest:

At the heart of every Video Keno machine is a Random Number Generator, often referred to as an RNG. The RNG is a clock operated computer chip that randomly selects preprogrammed read only memory (ROM) numbers. In this case they are numbers from 1 to 80.

When you make your wager you activate the Keno machine computer devices that are standing-by until you select your numbers, and push the start button. The RNG swings into action when the start button is pushed, randomly selecting numbers, and illuminating the playing screen with 20 computer-generated numbers between the number 1 and the number 80.

If the numbers you picked, and the random numbers generated by the RNG match, you get a Hit. If the number of Hits falls into the pay-table range, you win the appropriate number of credits listed on the pay-table.

For those of you that have played Video Keno, and chased the numbers from one side of the board to the other, the question always seems to arise; It appears that the machine is fixed to select numbers that I was playing after I moved to a different set of numbers, why is that?

I personally believe that some machines may be fixed and in today's environment of computer expertise, that could be easily done. These questions lead me to investigate as many State Gaming Standards and laws as I could, using the internet as a research tool.

In all of the states that I was able to gather information on, tampering with, or modifying RNG's is a violation of the gaming laws. Some states even have Loss of Gaming License as a penalty for intentionally modifying RNG's used in Video Poker or Video Keno to change the outcome of play.

I find it hard to believe a reputable casino would intentionally put their gaming license in jeopardy for the advantage of tampering with the machines RNG. They profit enough with the certified RNG's installed to take that chance.

Changing the payout numbers required to be matched by the player is the legal method most casinos use to vary the profitability of a particular machine. One of the key factors a player must look for before playing a particular machine is the required numbers to be matched for a payout. Even though it may appear identical to the machine next to it, the payout may be substantially less.

The question still remains; is the RNG fixed? It may be possible in casinos located outside of the United States, and casinos that are not under state regulations. We will explore the issue of When to Get Off a Machine later in the guide.

The next Chapter discusses the True Odds of Winning at Video Keno. This section is important to study as knowledge of the true odds will help you understand why we are hoping for the elusive nine out of nine or ten out of ten hit, but realistically should be playing for the six out of seven or the eight out of nine win that can be frequently accomplished.

CHAPTER 2

❀

True Odds of Winning

If you haven't seen the Statistical Odds of Hitting a Major Jackpot Payout on a Video Keno machine, hold on to your hat! The odds are huge, but the payouts are also huge versus the amount of money wagered. Carefully study the Odds Tables below, and we will then discuss the relevance to you as a winning player.

Note: I have not included Odds of Hitting tables for a two or three number play. Two and three number plays are possible on most Video Keno machines but the payout is quite small. Therefore, most Video Keno players do not usually play only two or three numbers.

If you were playing Live Keno in a casino lounge for five dollars a play, the payouts are substantial enough to make two or three number play worthwhile. I have included the numerical odds below for your reference:

- Odds of winning for a two number play are, 1 in 16.63. The Payout is, 15 for each credit wagered.

- Odds of winning for a three number play are, 1 in 72.07. The Payout is, 46 for each credit wagered.

The following **Odds of Hitting Tables** were taken from several internet sources and verified for accuracy:

Numbers Caught	Odds of Hitting
4 Numbers Picked	Odds*
4	1 in 326.43
3	1 in 23.12
2	1 in 4.70
1	1 in 2.31
0	1 in 3.24

*Odds are based on the standard 80 ball game, 20 balls drawn

Numbers Caught	Odds of Hitting
5 Numbers Picked	Odds*
5	1 in 1,550.57
4	1 in 82.70
3	1 in 11.91
2	1 in 3.70
1	1 in 2.46
0	1 in 4.40

*Odds are based on the standard 80 ball game, 20 balls drawn

Numbers Caught	Odds of Hitting
6 Numbers Picked	Odds*
6	1 in 7,752.84
5	1 in 323.03
4	1 in 35.04
3	1 in 7.70
2	1 in 3.24
1	1 in 2.75
0	1 in 6.00

*Odds are based on the standard 80 ball game, 20 balls drawn

Numbers Caught	Odds of Hitting
7 Numbers Picked	Odds*
7	1 in 40,979.31
6	1 in 1,365.98
5	1 in 115.76
4	1 in 19.16
3	1 in 5.71
2	1 in 3.06
1	1 in 3.17
0	1 in 8.22

*Odds are based on the standard 80 ball game, 20 balls drawn

Numbers Caught	Odds of Hitting
8 Numbers Picked	Odds*
8	1 in 230,114.60
7	1 in 6,232.27
6	1 in 422.53
5	1 in 54.64
4	1 in 12.27
3	1 in 4.65
2	1 in 3.05
1	1 in 3.75
0	1 in 11.33

*Odds are based on the standard 80 ball game, 20 balls drawn

Numbers Caught	Odds of Hitting
9 Numbers Picked	Odds*
9	1 in 1,380,687.65
8	1 in 30,681.95
7	1 in 1,690.11
6	1 in 174.84
5	1 in 30.67
4	1 in 8.76
3	1 in 4.06
2	1 in 3.16
1	1 in 4.53
0	1 in 15.67

*Odds are based on the standard 80 ball game, 20 balls drawn

Numbers Caught	Odds of Hitting
10 Numbers Picked	Odds*
10	1 in 8,911,711.18
9	1 in 163,381.37
8	1 in 7,384.47
7	1 in 620.68
6	1 in 87.11
5	1 in 19.44
4	1 in 6.79
3	1 in 3.74
2	1 in 3.39
1	1 in 5.57
0	1 in 21.84

*Odds are based on the standard 80 ball game, 20 balls drawn

After looking at the statistical odds, have you decided not to play Video Keno? I can't blame you if you have.

The first time I looked at the odds of winning at this game I also thought, why would I waste my money chasing such high odds? I concluded it was two things. The first was it did not cost much to play considering the other games in the casino. The second and most important reason was the payouts are HUGE relative to the amount of money wagered by the player.

You should also consider these things when you make a decision to play Video Keno or not. Most quarter slot machines take at least three quarters (or credits, regardless of the denomination) to win the highest payout on the machine. Odds of winning a $1000.00 jackpot on a standard quarter slot are about the same as winning seven out of seven on a

Video Keno machine, and it will cost you seventy-five cents each time you pull the handle. The seven out of seven win pay $1,750.00 and cost you only one quarter to play.

Let me ask you this question. How many $1000.00 (or more) slot machine jackpots have you won, and how much money did it really take to win it? My guess is, your true slot machine Jackpot Payouts have been rare. It has probably cost you over time, two, or three times the total amount paid by the slot machine to win it.

Using money management, closely checking the pay tables, and Blocking my numbers. I have won over **Seven Times** more money playing Video Keno than playing Slot Machines, or Video Poker in just the past six months!

Have I just been incredibly lucky? Possibly, but I have also used good player strategy, visual awareness of all the numbers displayed, and a touch of luck to make some very big wins playing Video Keno.

A point to remember is it only cost twenty-five cents a play on the Video Keno machine. It normally costs seventy-five cents, or even a dollar on some of the four-wheel slot machines to play.

In summary of the True Odds of Winning, be aware that winning ten out of ten is extremely rare. An eight out of nine, a seven out of seven, or a six out of six is quite common. The payback for a one-nickel or one-quarter (1 credit) is a worthwhile sum of money compared to a non-jackpot hit on a Slot Machine or Video Poker machine.

The next chapter outlines the correct Video Keno Pay Tables we are looking for when at the casino.

Continue reading the guide and, **COME HOME A WINNER!**

CHAPTER 3

❈

Pay Tables

In this Chapter, I will show you what Video Keno Pay Tables you should look for on a standard pay Video Keno Machine. In addition, what Video Keno Machines you should never play. The pay table displayed on the Video Keno machine always determines these facts.

Note: I have not included Pay Tables for a two or three number play. Two and three number plays are possible on most Video Keno machines but the payoff is quite small. Therefore, most Video Keno players do not frequently play only two or three numbers.

If you were playing Live Keno in a casino lounge for five dollars a play, the payouts are substantial enough to make two or three number play worthwhile. I have included the numerical payouts below for your reference:

- Payout for a two number play is 15 for each credit wagered. The odds of winning are, 1 in 16.63.

- Payout for a three number play is 46 for each credit wagered.

  The odds of winning are, 1 in 72.07.

The following Pay Tables are the correct Video Keno pay tables that we as **Winning Players** are looking for:

Pay Table:

4-Numbers Wagered	Credits Paid
Hit	Pay
1	0
2	2
3	5
4	91

Pay Table:

5-Numbers Wagered	Credits Paid
Hit	Pay
1	0
2	0
3	3
4	14
5	810

Pay Table:

6-Numbers Wagered	Credits Paid
Hit	Pay
1	0
2	0
3	3
4	4
5	70
6	1600

Pay Table:

7-Numbers Wagered	Credits Paid
Hit	Pay
1	0
2	0
3	1
4	2
5	21
6	400
7	7000

Pay Table:

8-Numbers Wagered	Credits Paid
Hit	Pay
1	0
2	0
3	0
4	2
5	12
6	98
7	1652
8	10,000

Pay Table:

9-Numbers Wagered	Credits Paid
Hit	Pay
1	0
2	0
3	0
4	1
5	6
6	44
7	335
8	4700
9	10,000

Pay Table:

10-Numbers Wagered	Credits Paid
Hit	Pay
1	0
2	0
3	0
4	0
5	5
6	24
7	142
8	1000
9	4500
10	10,000

After viewing and studying the above tables, we now need to learn how to find machines with the correct payouts we are looking for.

The primary machines that we will focus on are:

"IGT Game King" and "Bally Game Maker" Multifunction Video Keno Games.

By multifunction Video Keno games, we mean freestanding Video Keno machines that are capable of playing several different Video Keno games using the touch screen as a menu. As we mentioned previously, be aware, side-by-side machines that may look identical can have very different payout tables. On the "IGT Game King" and "Bally Game Maker" machines, it is quite easy to check the pay table using the following method:

On the touch screen, select "KENO" (the standard version keno). Then select "See Pay Table" menu.

Using what we will call the seven numbers scale, check the machine you are considering playing by paging down on the pay table menu for a seven number payout table. It should show 400 credits for a six out of seven win, and 7000 credits for a seven out of seven win.

These two numbers are the only numbers you need to consider when looking at the pay table menu. If these two numbers check out correctly, the rest of the pay tables shown in our pay table section will correspond. The denomination of the machine you are looking at is irrelevant. Whether it is a nickel, quarter, or dollar machine remember these numbers, six out of seven win = 400 credits, and seven out of seven win = 7000 credits with One Credit (or coin) played.

Note: Occasionally a "Bally Game Maker" machine will show the actual dollar pay out in dollar amounts. The payout on quarter machines should equal $100.00 for a six out of seven win and $1,750.00 for a seven out of seven win.

This is the first step to becoming a Winning Video Keno Player. Playing the correct machines with the correct pay tables is of the utmost importance!

CHAPTER 4

❀

Strategies and Play Samples

This section deals with strategy and play samples. Several different strategies should be used together in conjunction with player awareness and observation. The strategy topics we will talk about in this section are:

When to Get Off a Machine
Blocked Numbers
Strictly Vertical & Strictly Horizontal Numbers
Nine Blocks

Note: In this chapter, we will refer to the Video Keno Screen as the Board.

In the first chapter of the guide, we briefly mentioned when to get off a machine. One of the first things a player must do is make a quick observation of how the numbers are hitting.

The following explanation may help you to make a quick decision as to when you should get off a machine and move to another:

Most machines hit in numbered groups even though the numbers picked and displayed are picked by a Random Number Generator(RNG)if you watch closely even in the first few plays on a machine, this trend should be immediately visible. The machines we are looking for will be hitting in either blocked numbers or numbers that are running strictly horizontal or strictly vertical.

A machine that is spreading numbers in small groups of two or three numbers randomly is a machine to get off now, do not wait even 10 or 15 minutes! One of the most important things a player must do is respond to changing conditions on the board and make decisions quickly based on good play and strategy.

I have observed many players just sitting at a machine that is hitting numbers all over the board and playing either a straight-line pick or random picks of their own. Rarely will they hit pay table jackpots regardless of the amount of numbers they are playing. When you observe this type of action on the board for more than a few plays, it is time to move to another machine.

Note: Refer to Chapter 5 for strategy to deal with scattered numbers screen displays.

Don't forget, the most important thing we are here for is to "**To Win Money**" not for the joy of the game. If you are playing just because you love the game, do yourself a favor and buy a home computer C/D game with a virtual Keno game on it and save yourself a great deal of money. As I continue to say, "We are not playing in a real casino with our hard earned money to donate to the casino's operating budget". Do not go home a loser because you just love to play Keno.

Random Hit machines will not give us the winning combination of pay out numbers that we are looking for.

Blocked Numbers:

When we refer to blocked numbers, we are looking for numbers spread across the board in groups of four or more numbers that run in rows or columns, vertically or horizontally. This is usually apparent to the player quite quickly after starting play at a machine. See the following example:

Blocked Numbers Vertical & Horizontal

The sample below shows twenty numbers selected by the Random Number Generator in several groups of numbers. The first group of numbers on the top section of the board is eleven numbers that are in a group, running mostly vertical, with several numbers in a horizontal pattern.

The bottom board has nine numbers that are also mostly vertical with a small group that are horizontal. The player should be looking for patterns of numbers generated that are vertical and horizontal but most importantly as shown in this example, numbers that are in block's or groups of three or more numbers.

Using the example below, after one or two similar groups of numbers have been shown by the machine. The player needs to move quickly marking a vertical of horizontal block of numbers ranging from six numbers to ten numbers. My favorite selection of numbers is a Seven Spot or a Nine Spot.

1	2	3	4	5	6	7	8	9	10
11	12	13	14	15	16	17	18	19	20
21	22	23	24	25	26	27	28	29	30
31	32	33	34	35	36	37	38	39	40
41	42	43	44	45	46	47	48	49	50
51	52	53	54	55	56	57	58	59	60
61	62	63	64	65	66	67	68	69	70
71	72	73	74	75	76	77	78	79	80

Playing Seven Blocked Numbers:

The example below shows a series of seven player numbers selected and blocked vertically:

1	2	3	4	5	6	7	8	9	10
11	12	13	X	15	16	17	18	19	20
21	22	23	X	X	26	27	28	29	30
31	32	33	X	X	36	37	38	39	40
41	42	43	X	X	46	47	48	49	50
51	52	53	54	55	56	57	58	59	60
61	62	63	64	65	66	67	68	69	70
71	72	73	74	75	76	77	78	79	80

PLAYER NUMBERS "BLOCKED VERTICAL"
"7 SPOT PICKED"

The example below shows a series of seven player numbers selected and blocked horizontally:

1	2	3	4	5	6	7	8	9	10
11	12	13	X	X	X	X	18	19	20
21	22	23	24	X	X	X	28	29	30
31	32	33	34	35	36	37	38	39	40

41	42	43	44	45	46	47	48	49	50
51	52	53	54	55	56	57	58	59	60
61	62	63	64	65	66	67	68	69	70
71	72	73	74	75	76	77	78	79	80

PLAYER NUMBERS "BLOCKED HORIZONTAL"
"7 SPOT PICKED"

Playing Nine Blocked Numbers:

The example below shows a series of nine player numbers selected and blocked vertically:

1	2	3	4	5	6	7	8	9	10
11	12	13	X	X	16	17	18	19	20
21	22	23	X	X	26	27	28	29	30
31	32	33	X	X	36	37	38	39	40
41	42	43	X	X	46	47	48	49	50
51	52	53	X	55	56	57	58	59	60
61	62	63	64	65	66	67	68	69	70
71	72	73	74	75	76	77	78	79	80

PLAYER NUMBERS "BLOCKED VERTICAL"
"9 SPOT PICKED"

There are two distinct methods of play for blocked numbers. I have observed both methods working well and have argued the point of my preference of course in a friendly way:

Method 1: Stay put on the board regardless of the trend of the machine.

Method 2: Move your block as the machine makes selections and moves the RNG selected blocks randomly around the board.

My friend Glena, who is a regular player at "Mystic Lake Casino" just southwest of Minneapolis Minnesota, is an advocate of the Stay Put Method. What this means is Glena plays a block of numbers (usually seven, eight or nine numbers) and positions them on the board pretty much in the same place every time she plays. She rarely moves them during the entire course of that days play. The important thing is Glena plays blocks, and groups of numbers. She occasionally will play a strictly vertical or strictly horizontal set of numbers (which we will talk about later in this section) and is very successful. Glena's point of view, which differs from mine is, "set your numbers and blocks and let the machine picks come to you". I differ in this viewpoint and this has evoked some lively but friendly discussions on the subject.

My personal preference is to set up blocks either vertically or horizontal depending upon the machine. Then move the block to another place on the board after two or three unsuccessful plays. Again, this is my own preference (partly due to lack of patience) and both will be successful if the major rule is always followed. Set Up Blocks of Numbers either vertically or horizontally on the board.

Rule Number 3:

Always use Vertical or Horizontal Blocks of Numbers regardless of the amount of numbers you are wagering. There is one exception to this rule, and it is when:

The board is showing a Scattered Screen Presentation of numbers consistently. Refer to Chapter 5 for the correct strategy for scattered number screen presentations.

Playing a Strictly Vertical or Strictly Horizontal board:

I mentioned in an earlier section the method of playing strictly vertical or strictly horizontal number patterns. When you set your blocks, regardless of how many numbers you play watch closely during the course of play for a machine presentation that is showing continuous rows of numbers that are running in groups of four or more numbers in a vertical or horizontal pattern as shown below:

1	2	3	4	5	6	7	8	9	10
11	12	13	14	15	16	17	18	19	20
21	22	23	24	25	26	27	28	29	30
31	32	33	34	35	36	37	38	39	40
41	42	43	44	45	46	47	48	49	50
51	52	53	54	55	56	57	58	59	60
61	62	63	64	65	66	67	68	69	70
71	72	73	74	75	76	77	78	79	80

Screen Presentaion with
"Strict Vertical Block"

In this example the four column is showing a vertical run of seven numbers.

Watching the board closely for vertical or horizontal runs of numbers that continue to repeat in a certain column or row is a good way to pick up a quick win.

In the following example the sixty row is showing a horizontal run of eight numbers:

1	2	3	4	5	6	7	8	9	10
11	12	13	14	15	16	17	18	19	20
21	22	23	24	25	26	27	28	29	30
31	32	33	34	35	36	37	38	39	40
41	42	43	44	45	46	47	48	49	50
51	52	53	54	55	56	57	58	59	60
61	62	63	64	65	66	67	68	69	70
71	72	73	74	75	76	77	78	79	80

Screen Presentaion with
"Strict Horizontal Block"

It is very important that you watch the board closely and not lose the opportunity to make a quick change from your normal block play to a strictly vertical or horizontal play strategy.

Just to keep you sharp, go back to the first chapter of the guide and look at the graphic showing Seven Numbers Played ("6 Hits = 400 Credits"). I hope you see a very good horizontal run on the Thirty Row. The numbers 33 to 38 are all illuminated in a row. Now that you know what to look for be ready to make that quick switch.

I mentioned my friend Glena that plays eight numbers quite regularly. She always positions the eight numbers she selects on the left or right vertical column or the top horizontal row or bottom horizontal row. Is she successful? Absolutely, and that helps fire our discussions on staying put once you have set your numbers. I guess I can't argue with success, but I just can't sit there all evening playing the same row or column time after time. As I mentioned several times, the important thing is she always plays a block of numbers, even though we disagree on the method of play. After reading this guide, I want YOU to be flexible, aware of trends on the board, and able to take advantage of opportunities as they appear.

CHAPTER 5

❀

"Hot"-"Hot"-"Hot"

This chapter was developed and included just days before the guide was published. I titled it "Hot"-"Hot"-"Hot" because it deals with the subject of strategy for winning when the machine consistently displays a Scattered Number Screen Presentation. A scattered number screen presentation is an extremely difficult presentation for consistently winning at Video Keno. I believe the following strategy is a real breakthrough to consistently winning money at Video Keno.

To be honest, I could not let this guide go to publication without including this new information. Hence, the title of the chapter "Hot"-"Hot"-"Hot".

Before we go any further let me define a Scattered Number Screen Presentation:

A scattered number screen presentation is if the machine continually presents very small blocks of two or three numbers. They may even be single number presentations randomly distributed around the top and bottom half of the screen.

This effectively negates the strategy of playing blocks of six, seven, eight, or more numbers, and can be not only be frustrating to deal with, but expensive. Your blocks of selected numbers will only get one or two hits per play. This will not give you enough hits for a break even payout and will deplete your playing credits quickly.

Several of my friends and I that play regularly developed the strategy below over time. After discussing the subject almost daily over the past six months, we all came to the same conclusion; a scattered number screen presentation is presented to the player repeatedly throughout the game and on some machines, it may be present the entire session of play.

The problem is actually two fold for the player. One there may not be another machine you can to move too, and secondly, your playing credits will quickly be depleted without some small wins, or break-even payouts.

All made an observation: The small two and three groups of numbers presented by the machine were often grouped in the top and bottom corners of the screen, the left or right side of the screen at mid level, and even on occasion the top center and bottom center of the screen.

I worked on this anomaly for several months by splitting my numbers when the machine continually presented scattered number presentations. The results were consistent enough to add this section and define a new strategy that may help you win more often.

Follow the strategy below and pick up a few wins when most players can't!

Strategy for winning when the machine is consistently presenting Scattered Numbers:

Our normal selection of numbers to play is six to ten numbers, grouped tightly together in either horizontal or vertical blocks of numbers. On a machine that is, presenting blocks either vertical or horizontally in groups of five, six, or even seven numbers, this is a good strategy to play. This method of play should net you some substantial wins.

Occasionally throughout the playing session, the machine will present scattered numbers of two or three numbers that are randomly spread across the upper and lower half of the screen. As we pointed out in the above section this will effectively negate your large blocks of numbers and often not hit enough of your block numbers to score a break-even win on the pay table.

When confronted with the problem it is a good time to move too a scattered number strategy and break up your blocks of numbers in the following ways:

If you were playing seven numbers, the correct strategy for a Seven Number Setup on a scattered screen would be as follows:

1. Select 79, 80, and 70 the three right bottom corner numbers on the screen.

2. Select number 1 and 2 at the top left corner of the screen.

3. Select number 9 and 10 at the top right corner of the screen.

The above selection of numbers will give you a small block of numbers in the bottom right corner, two numbers on the top left corner, and two numbers in the top right corner of the screen.

The benefit of this number setup is that you can now take advantage of the scattered screen presentation that is being generated by the machine.

My recommendation with this setup is to stay with the initial selection of numbers and occasionally move the bottom right block of numbers (79,80 and 70) to the bottom left corner of the screen using the numbers (61, 71 and 72). Continue with this setup strategy until the screen presentation returns to our preferred large block sets of numbers.

The small blocks of numbers you are setting up can also be moved to the top and bottom of the screen. Select the numbers 5, 6,15,65,66, and 75, 76. This selection will give you a small block of three numbers in the top half of the screen and a block of four numbers in the bottom half of the screen.

If you were playing nine numbers, the correct strategy for a Nine Number Setup on a scattered screen would be as follows:

1. Using the top row as your base line, select 9, 10, 19 and 20 as a 4 number block on the top right side of the screen.

2. Add numbers 1, 2, 3, 11, and 12 for a 5 number block on the top left corner of the screen.

   Note: Refer to any of the screen graphics contained in the guide for a number reference that applies to the above information.

As the scattered screen presentation changes, move your blocks of numbers from the top to the bottom. You may also keep one block in the top half of the screen and move the other to the bottom half of the screen as necessary. You can also vary you number selection between seven or nine numbers as you move the blocks around the screen trying to catch a favorable group of numbers. This should at least keep you in the pay table range, minimizing your losses. Continue this varying of number selections until the screen returns to more favorable block presentation of numbers.

When playing a small number setup you should move the blocks of numbers frequently for the best opportunity to pick up a win. Remember, the screen is presenting a scattered number presentation that moves from top to bottom, and side to side randomly. The object of our strategy is to be in the right place at the right time to pick up a six, or even a seven number win.

I have personally picked up a seven out of seven win for a sizable jackpot ($1,750.00) and an eight out of nine win for a smaller ($1,175.00) jackpot using this strategy.

The above tips and strategy are an advanced method of play to maintain your playing credits, while waiting out a Scattered Number Screen Presentation.

CHAPTER 6

❁

Summary and Play Tips

This chapter provides a summary of highlights of the previous topics covered with some additional detail and play tips that will help you walk away from the casino **A WINNER**.

The first and most important rule is; always check the pay tables of the machine that you are going to play before you play it. I cannot emphasize enough how important it is for you to take this first step before dropping even one nickel into a Video Keno machine. Remember, the machine you are playing, and the machine right next to it can have tremendously different pay tables. This could cost you hundreds of dollars on a big number win, but possibly even thousands of dollars lost on that elusive "Jack Pot Win".

Look for "Game King Multifunction Video Keno" or "Bally Game Maker" machines. They have the most consistent payouts nationwide and match the jackpot payouts we are looking for.

Remember the seven-number rule; always check the pay table for seven numbers played. Look for a payout of, 400 (or more) credits for a six out of seven win, and 7000 credits paid for a seven out of seven win. If you find these two key numbers, the rest of the pay tables on that machine will fall in place.

A smart player is a good player. When you finish this chapter, it would probably be a good time to go back and refresh yourself with the

Pay Tables in Chapter 3, particularly if you are on your way to a casino. Know the payouts so you can play smart and get that Big Win.

Bally Game Maker machines vs. IGT Game King machines:
Bally Game Maker machines look very similar to the IGT Game King machines, and play identically. They sometimes have slightly lower bottom end payouts, but the high-end payouts on most of the machines I have checked match the "IGT Game King" machines. The loss is fairly minimal on the standard pay machines and is not a reason to avoid them. I would recommend play on either machine.

"0" Hit Payout Machines:
The IGT Game King and the Bally Game Maker both offer "0" Hit Payout machines. **Do not play ANY Video Keno machines that have a zero hit payout.**
Here is how they work and why you should not play them:
"0" hit machines pay an equal amount of credits to your original wager if you do not hit any numbers picked. For example, if you pick six numbers and do not hit any of the six numbers selected, the machine credits you back the amount of your original wager.
The problem is, the "0" hit payback does not come into effect unless you play five or more numbers. The pay table below is an example of a "0" hit pay table.

Pay Table:

6 -Numbers Wagered	Credits Paid
Hit	Pay
0	1
1	0
2	0
3	3
4	4
5	50
6	625

Two things are working against you on this type of machine, with this pay table. The foremost being, the payout for mid number wins and even the jackpot win for six out of six is extremely low along with the already high odds against winning. It is also highly unlikely that you will not hit any numbers when playing at least six numbers to receive the even money payout.

Notice the six out of six-jackpot payout on the table shown above. The payout amount is only 625 credits for a jackpot win of six out of six vs. the standard payout of 1600 credits for six out of six win as shown in Chapter 3. The standard payout on a quarter machine would be $400.00 for this particular jackpot vs. the "0" hit machines jackpot of only $151.23.

This is a substantial difference in pay back return and should be reason enough on it's own to avoid these machines. Remember it is no more difficult to win a six out of six on a standard play machine than it is on a "0" hit machine. Why not reap the benefit of the additional jackpot money paid!

In summary of the "0" hit machines:

Always avoid this type of machine. Personally, if the standard payout machines in the casino were full, I would wait for a favorable machine with a standard payout. I may even go to another casino before I would play the "0" hit type Video Keno machines. I recommend you do the same.

International Gaming Technology (IGT) keypad machines:

These are the older style Video Keno machines with a small video screen and a touchpad located under the screen. It is similar to a computer keyboard (and just for us "older folks", it looks like a typewriter key board).

I have not previously mentioned the older IGT machines for one reason; many of the newer casinos do not have them for the sheer reason that they are difficult to get. Although many of the older casinos and some of the smaller casinos in Las Vegas still have them.

Many people still like to play them, and the pay tables are comparable to the newer IGT Game King machines. They are fun to play with the traditional "Ding-Ding-Ding" sound they make as the RNG selects and places the numbers on the screen. For the most part, they are good pay-out machines. Do not be afraid to play them if you come across them and the new "IGT Game King" or "Bally Game Maker" machines are not available.

When to get off a machine:

Get off a machine when the machine is not blocking numbers and showing only scattered random numbers. When you start playing a new machine, watch very closely in the first few minutes of play for random or blocked numbers being presented. Sometimes you may have to play a few rounds to evaluate the patterns shown.

Set up your blocks as we discussed in Chapter 4, but make only minimum wagers during this time. In a reasonable amount of time, you should be able to see the patterns of a blocking machine, or a random machine. If the patterns are still random, leave the machine and look for a blocking machine. Do not sit at a machine all day hoping it will change. Make your move quickly to conserve money. Your chances of winning will be greatly increased.

Note: If all the machines are, full or you feel you are seeing only Scattered Number Screen Presentations on the machines available to you. Refer to Chapter 5 "Hot"-"Hot"-"Hot" and use the strategy learned there to deal with scattered number screen presentations.

Varying the amount of numbers you select vs. the amount of the wager:

Depending upon the wager you are making, some selections of numbers such as betting seven numbers vs. betting nine numbers can become an important issue. Let's look at a one-nickel and one-quarter wager and see what sets of numbers are the best to play and why.

If you are making a one-nickel wager, play a six number or nine number set for the following reasons:

A six out of six win on a one-nickel wager pays $80.00 and is not too hard to hit. If you were playing seven numbers, a six out of seven win only pays $20.00 on a one-nickel wager. Most people will not be satisfied with only a $20.00 win, and will put it back into the machine before they leave.

A nine number selection played on a one-nickel wager is a very good wager to play for the following reasons:

A seven out of nine is hit quite often for $16.90 which gives you some playing money and an eight of nine win will pay an incredible $235.00 for a one-nickel wager. The eight of nine win is tough to hit, but is done often, and the payback is an enormous amount for the bet wagered. I have seen very few nine out of nine wins, but in this case, the payout would be an astounding $500.00 for only a one-nickel wager.

If you are making a one-quarter wager, play a seven number or nine number set for the following reasons:

If you play seven numbers for a one-quarter wager, a six out of seven win will net you $100.00 (400 credits), and is a very good return on a one-quarter wager. The unique thing about a six out of seven win is it can be hit quite often. I have personally hit six out of seven twice in a row, followed by a seven out of seven win within a few minutes on the same machine.

Hitting a seven out of seven can be tough, but when you do, you will net $1,750.00 for a one-quarter wager (using our preferred payout tables). This is a huge jackpot for the amount invested and is why we are playing Video Keno vs. Standard Slot Machines!

I mentioned above that nine numbers played is also a good block of numbers to play for a quarter wager. Here is why:

A six out of nine win nets you $11.00 dollars and gives you extra playing money and time on the machine. A seven out of nine win pays $83.75. That is a tidy sum, and can be won quite easily and sometimes fairly often. That can add up quickly.

An eight out of nine win, short of hitting the jackpot, is what we are looking for on this particular choice of numbers to play.

The payout on a standard pay machine for an eight out of nine win with a quarter wagered is $1,175.00 (4700 credits) and is a very substantial jackpot. In most states, this win is just under the taxable withholding limit of $1,200.00. Of course as in all gambling winnings, you are responsible to file the proper tax documentation for the win.

Playing the nickel machines vs. the quarter machines has some advantages above and beyond the obvious; that it costs less to play. If you play three nickels or three credits instead of just one-nickel, a seven out of seven win pays $1050.00, which is really a nice jackpot for only a fifteen-cent wager, and again, it is just under the taxable withholding amount of $1200.00. An eight out of nine jackpot will pay $705.00 with fifteen cents wagered and is certainly worth playing for, particularly since it is not that difficult to get.

The nickel machines will give you more play time, and at this game, the more time you can spend on the machine the better chance you have of hitting what I call; A Big Hit.

Splitting your picks into small blocks of numbers:

Occasionally you will run across a machine that is presenting small strips of numbers in blocks of three or four lines or columns evenly spaced between the top and bottom of the screen. This machine is an excellent machine to quickly make an exception to the blocks only rule and play what I call top and bottom split number picks.

For example, mark a small block of three numbers in the top half of the machine connected together either in a vertical or horizontal row or column. Continue by marking a small block of four numbers connected together either in a vertical or horizontal row or column in the lower half of the screen. This will give you a split number screen with three in the top and four in the bottom. The total numbers marked will be seven.

Larger amounts up to a nine number pick five in the top and four in the bottom half of the screen or smaller amounts down to a six number pick three in the top and three in the bottom half of the screen can also be played with considerable success.

When you see this type of screen presentation quickly take advantage of it. Many times a seven out of seven or even a nine out of nine can be picked up quickly. This phenomenon does not happen often and may only last a few minutes.

Remember; be flexible, observant, and ready to change strategy quickly.

Note: Refer to Chapter 5 for play strategy to deal with a scattered number screen display, which is different from the above.

Now for what I call the Big Shooters, who have the budget to make one-dollar or more wagers time after time.

The payout is huge for the dollar plus gamer. Although you need to keep in mind, sometimes this game can take many coins, time after time, without a substantial payout and lends itself to the smaller wagering patient player.

I saw a woman the other evening at the casino that reinforced the belief I have for not making large wagers at this game. She had just made a nice win, picking six out of six for a $2,000.00 payout. She had won it about a half an hour earlier that evening.

She was playing a nickel machine for 30 credits; $1.50 at a time and was trying for a second big win of six out of six on the same numbers she had just won on. I did take note that she was a block number player and was playing them correctly. I sat there drinking my coffee and continued to play my one-nickel bets watching her.

She dropped most of the two thousand dollars she won right back into the machine in $100.00 bills, playing 30 credits at a time. She continued to play 30 credits each play, and believe me, those one-hundred dollar bills kept going right back into that machine. Within a half an hour, she had lost most of the $2,000.00 dollars she had just won.

When making large wagers your capital funds and for that matter your 401K fund can go into these machines quickly when you hit a dry spell. When you hit, you will hit very big playing seven, eight, nine, or even ten numbers. If you do not win more often than not you will lose big!

My advise; even if you have the one-dollar or more budget, play light, win some good pay backs and most of all have fun without making the casino rich.

Progressive Jackpot Video Keno machines:

Progressive jackpots are quite alluring when the jackpots often reach into the hundred thousand dollar category. My advise, watch the low end payouts to be sure you are not getting hurt too bad, block your numbers, look for patterns, and go for it! A couple hundred thousand dollar jackpot payout for a twenty-five or fifty cent wager is tough to find anywhere!

The next Chapter I named "Seven Rules to Win With". Read them carefully and take at least one of them committed to memory each time you go to the casino. It will not be long and you will be able to take all of them with you, making you not only an informed player, but also a smart player that will win money.

CHAPTER 7

❀

The Seven Rules to Win With

The final Chapter focuses on player rules that you can reference and memorize to help you become a winning Video Keno player.

Pick out one of the "the seven rules to win with" each time before you go to the casino, and simply take it with you. Soon you will have all the winning rules memorized:

Rule #1: Always check the Pay Tables on the machine before you begin play:

Look for the seven number rule payout; it should be 400 credits for a six out of seven win and 7000 credits for a seven out of seven jackpot win. Do not play for a lower payout unless it is a large progressive jackpot. At that point; it's your call to play or not.

Rule #2: Know when to get off a machine:

Random Hit machines will generally not give the winning combination of pay out numbers that you are looking for. If a machine is continuously hitting randomly around the board get off the machine and find a winning machine that is hitting in blocks.

Note: If it's not possible to change machines, remember the strategy in Chapter 5 on how to deal with scattered number screen presentations.

Rule # 3: Always use Vertical or Horizontal Blocks of Numbers regardless of the amount of numbers you are wagering:

Refer to Chapter 4 of the guide if necessary that shows you how to lay out vertical or horizontal blocks of numbers. Stick with it the blocks should payoff.

The one exception to this rule is if the machine is running strictly vertical or strictly horizontal. Move your play numbers to split numbers accordingly in a strictly vertical or strictly horizontal position as shown in the Winning Strategies and Play Sample Chapter 4.

Rule #4: Look for IGT Game King Multifunction Video Keno machines and Bally Game Maker machines:

The IGT Game King and Bally Game Maker machines usually offer the payouts you are looking for. There are other type machines that also offer satisfactory payouts such as the older IGT (International Game Technology) machines, but are some times difficult to find.

Rule #5: Never play a machine that has a "0" hit payout:

The "0" hit payout option can reduce a jackpot hit to as little as one-third the normal payout. For the nominal savings it's not worth it in the long run.

Rule #6: Tailor the numbers you bet to match your wager:

Tailor the amount of numbers you play to the amount of your wager. For example if you play on a nickel machine using one credit per play, bet nine numbers for a $230.00 win on a eight out of nine hit or possibly a $500.00 win for a nine out of nine hit. If you only play seven numbers and hit a six of seven the payout is $20.00. Most people will not be happy with a $20.00 payout and drop it right back in the machine trying for a seven out of seven hit.

If you play on a quarter machine one credit per play, bet seven numbers, for the following reason, a six out of seven will then pay $100.00, which you should take and leave the casino for the day. A seven out of seven hit pays $1750.00 a jackpot win for the day. Keep in mind the tax advantages of some of the other wagers we talked about in Summary and Play Tips, Chapter 6 of the guide.

Rule #7: Money Management:

Never wager more money toward a possible win than the win itself.

This means don't play $200.00 as a daily stake to try to win a $150.00 jackpot. You only need look around your nearest casino to see how many people are ignorant of this basic rule of money management.

Use money management every time you go to the casino. Take with you only your playing session money, which is the total amount of money you plan to wager with for the day. Leave the ATM and credit card at home. If you make a substantial hit leave the casino for the day and leave a winner not a loser.

The final and most important un-written rule is; "never doubt that over the long run, the casino will **ALWAYS** be the winner". If you win a substantial jackpot, leave the casino. Come back to win again another day!

GOOD LUCK AND WIN BIG!

Authors footnote:
I welcome your comments regarding the guide you just read and would very much like to hear from you "win or lose" via e-mail at my web site. Please contact me at **www.kenowinner.com** and I will try to respond to all comments.